Little Ella grew up in New York. She had a beautiful voice and loved music.

When she was old enough, Ella went to a strict school. She didn't like it. So, she ran away ...

… and made a living singing
and dancing on the streets.

FRUiT

AMATEUR NIGH
AMATEUR N
1st
2nd
3rd

One evening, she entered a singing competition. She won first prize!

That night, Ella was so excited she couldn't sleep. She imagined herself on a big stage!

It wasn't long before Ella got her first singing job. She toured the country with a big band.

NEVADA
FLORIDA
WHITE ONLY

Ella never sang a song the same way twice. She turned somersaults with her voice.

She made up new sounds on the spot. Sometimes she invented new words, like "Dubi-dubi-dubu-daba"...

W E
P P
I
O P

… and she sang slow songs as sweet as lullabies.

Eventually, Ella decided it was time to go solo.

The best musicians in
the world wanted to
play with her.

The Complete Ella Fitzgerald Song Books
ELLA GERSHW
ELLA & LOUIS AGAIN
VOL.2
ella
SUNSHIN
OF YOUR LOV

Ella sang everything,
from bop to swing.
Her voice swooped
and soared until the
day she retired.

And that's how little Ella,
the girl who loved music,
became the First Lady of Song.

My First **Ella Fitzgerald**
Little People, **BIG DREAMS**

Ella Fitzgerald

Introduce your baby to the pioneering jazz singer.

Told in simple sentences, this young reader edition of the best-selling series is perfect to read out loud to little dreamers.

This board book edition first published in 2019 by
Frances Lincoln Children's Books, an imprint of
The Quarto Group. 400 First Avenue North, Suite 400, Minneapolis, MN 55401, USA.
T (0)20 7700 6700 F (0)20 7700 8066 **www.QuartoKnows.com**
Original hardback edition first published in Spain in 2017 by Alba Editorial, s.l.u. www.albaeditorial.com.

Published by Rachel Williams. Designed by Karissa Santos. Edited by Katy Flint. Production by Catherine Cragg.
Manufactured in ShaoGuan, China SL032019
9 7 5 3 2 4 6 8

50899
9 781786 032577
$8.99 US
$11.99 CAN
£5.99 UK
Frances Lincoln Children's Books
www.franceslincoln.com